I AM
A
WRITER

Copyright Page

I Am a Writer

Copyright © 2021 by LaMonda A Sykes

All rights reserved. Printed in the United States of America. No part of this book may be used or reproduced in any manner whatsoever without written permission except in the case of brief quotations embodied in critical articles or reviews.

ISBN: 978-1-7339337-7-3

First Edition: December 2021

For more information contact:

With a Capital M Publishing Group, LLC

Po Box 52656

Durham, NC 27717

http://www.withacapitalm.com

Book and Cover design by With a Capital M Publishing Group, LLC

Photo Credit: Suave Visions

Graphics provided by Canva.com

This book is dedicated to my grandparents: Clifton and Lessie Baker; Edward and Frances Sykes. Thank you for always believing in me. May you continue to rest in peace.

Author's Message

The life we want to create lies on the tip of our tongue. However, for us to see what we speak, we must believe.

Oh, trust me, it's easier said than done-- especially when you (I mean me) don't know how the world will receive your gift.

But it doesn't matter what the world thinks! You are who **you** say you are. You are full of purpose, and one person is waiting on you to fulfill the burning desire inside you! Don't keep them waiting...

I genuinely pray that these next thirty days are transformative for you. I declare that your belief is restored with every affirmation and reflection. I pray your completed project exceeds your expectations and restores faith in this world!

Enjoy the journey, my friend!

With love,

LaMload

I am doing this, period!

Reflection

My story will inspire someone to tell their story.

Reflection

My legacy is stitched in the pages of my project.

Reflection

I permit myself to be as vulnerable as I need to.

Reflection

Social standards will not censor my words.

Reflection

Love will be birthed from my pen.

Reflection

My story lies at the end of my pen.

Reflection

Writing is my superpower.

Reflection

My words will save someone's world.

Reflection

With:

One word.

One line.

One page.

I will complete my project.

Reflection

No one can tell my story as well as I can.

Reflection

Mistakes mean I am trying.

Reflection

My past does not define my future... but it made a great story!

Reflection

I. Trust. God (repeat 3x slowly).

Reflection

It's not a typo—-it's creative expression. (Don't beat yourself up, just make the change.)

Reflection

I AM A WRITER

Reflection

I'm holding myself accountable to finish my project.

Reflection

I believe in me.

Reflection

Creativity flows naturally to me.

Reflection

I am proud of all I've accomplished.

Reflection

I have a scheduled time to write.
No outside distractions are allowed.

Reflection

Every day, I become a better writer.

Reflection

Taking a break isn't quitting. I will finish.

Reflection

I am trusting the process.

Reflection

Writing comes naturally.

Reflection

I am prepared for the success of my project.

Reflection

I am grateful for the provision to bring this project to life.

Reflection

I embrace my present.
I am thankful for my past.
I am hopeful for the future.

Reflection

My one day is now!

Reflection

I find inspiration in everything.

Reflection

www.ingramcontent.com/pod-product-compliance
Lightning Source LLC
Chambersburg PA
CBHW071254070526
44583CB00017B/2464